Weatherwise

Sunshine and Drought

Kate Purdie

PowerKiDS press

New York

Published in 2010 by The Rosen Publishing Group Inc.
29 East 21st Street, New York, NY 10010

First Edition

Design: Rob Norridge and Paul Myerscough
Editor: Sarah Eason
Editor for Wayland: Claire Shanahan
Illustrations: Geoff Ward
Photography by Tudor Photography
Picture research: Maria Joannou
Consultant: Harold Pratt

Library of Congress Cataloging-in-Publication Data

Purdie, Kate.
Sunshine and drought / Kate Purdie.
p. cm. – (Weatherwise)
Includes index.
ISBN 978-1-61532-266-4 (library binding)
ISBN 978-1-61532-278-7 (paperback)
ISBN 978-1-61532-280-0 (6-pack)
1. Sunshine–Juvenile literature. 2. Droughts–Juvenile literature. I. Title.
QC911.2.P87 2010
551.5'271–dc22
2009026806

Photographs:
Corbis: Dean Conger 13, Gabe Palmer 6, Caroline Penn 25, Reuters 23;
Dreamstime: Ron Chapple Studios 1, 22; Getty Images: The Image Bank/Peter Lilja 12,
Photographers Choice/Vladimir Pcholkin 11; Istockphoto: Brasil2 18; Rex Features:
David Heerde 9, Peter Macdiarmid 24, Eye Ubiquitous 26; Shutterstock: Galina Barskaya 10,
Geanina Bechea 15, Jules Kitano 20, Mypokcik 4, Orientaly 14, Pixpax 17, Norman Pogson 8,
Jeremy Richards 21, Svemir 19, Suzanne Tucker 27; Still Pictures: Mark Edwards 16.

Cover photograph: Corbis (Gabe Palmer)

Manufactured in China
CPSIA Compliance Information: Batch #WAW0102PK: For Further Information
contact Rosen Publishing, New York, New York at 1-800-237-9932

Contents

What is sunshine?

Sunshine is the light and heat that comes from the Sun. Sometimes, it is possible to see sunshine reaching the Earth as rays of light called sunbeams. Sunshine is part of weather. Weather describes the conditions outdoors at a particular time—for example, if it is raining or windy.

All living things on Earth need the Sun's light and heat to live. Without the Sun's heat, the world would be too cold for people and animals to survive.

Without sunlight, crops such as these grapes would not be able to grow and there would be nothing for people and animals to eat.

Sun

Sun's rays

Earth

The Sun's rays travel through space to reach the Earth.

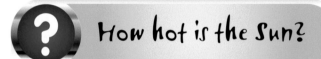

? How hot is the Sun?

At its center, the Sun is 27 million degrees Fahrenheit (15 million degrees Celsius)—20,000 times hotter than the hottest volcano on Earth. Just enough of the Sun's heat reaches the Earth to make the planet warm enough for life to exist.

The Sun's heat and light affect people every day. For example, if it is hot and sunny, people might stay outside. People might wear clothes such as T-shirts and shorts that keep them cool.

A sunny world

The Sun shines everywhere in the world—for at least part of the time! The Earth moves around the Sun in the sky. Depending on where the Earth is in the sky, and where people live, it will be either day or night. The amount of sunshine places receive changes with the **seasons**—fall, winter, spring, and summer. These are periods of the year when the weather changes.

The beaches of Brisbane, Australia, have between six and seven hours of sunshine every day in the summer.

The map shows that droughts occur most in Africa.

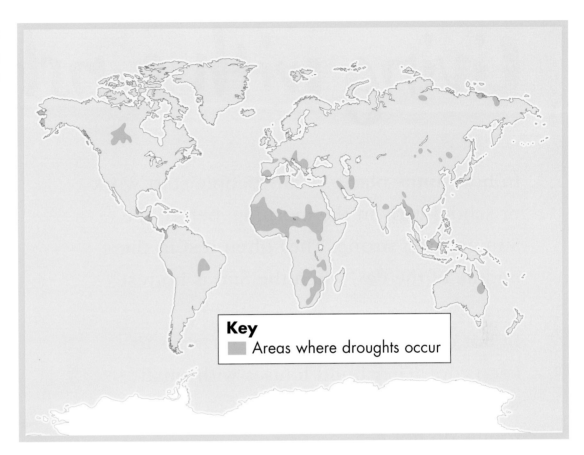

Key
Areas where droughts occur

In some countries, it is sunnier at different times of the year. In the United States (U.S.A.) and the United Kingdom (U.K.), the Sun is stronger in the summer than it is in the winter. In other countries, such as Brazil, in South America, the Sun is strong all year round.

Some parts of the world are sunnier than others. Some places are so sunny that droughts occur. This is when rain does not fall for a several months or more.

Unbelievable!

The sunniest place in the world is Yuma, Arizona. It has 4,055 hours of sunshine a year.

Living with sunshine

In hot, sunny places, many people start work or school early in the morning, before the Sun gets too strong. They often rest in the middle of the day, when the Sun is hottest.

In hot countries, people look for ways to keep cool. They build houses with small windows, so that rooms do not get too warm. They use fans to make a cool breeze. In rich countries, such as the United States, people use **air conditioning** in buildings to lower the temperature.

Closing window shutters helps to keep houses cool in many hot countries.

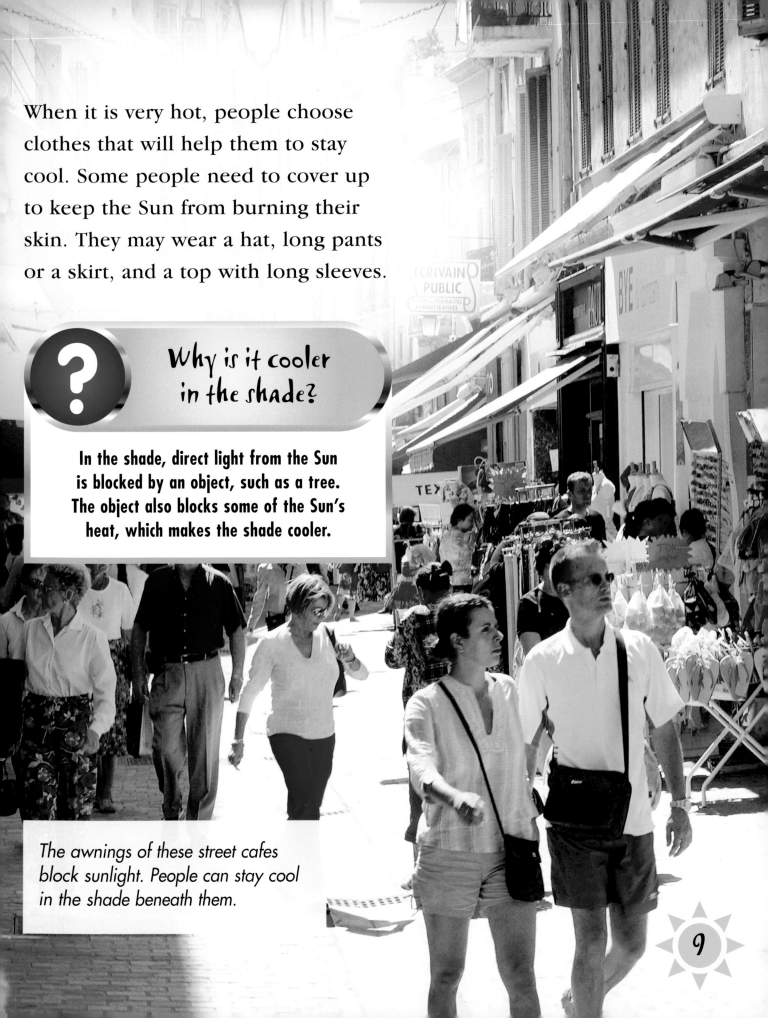

When it is very hot, people choose clothes that will help them to stay cool. Some people need to cover up to keep the Sun from burning their skin. They may wear a hat, long pants or a skirt, and a top with long sleeves.

? Why is it cooler in the shade?

In the shade, direct light from the Sun is blocked by an object, such as a tree. The object also blocks some of the Sun's heat, which makes the shade cooler.

The awnings of these street cafes block sunlight. People can stay cool in the shade beneath them.

Fun with sunshine

Many people enjoy spending time in the sunshine. They may go on vacation to sunny places, where they can play and relax on the beach, and cool off in the sea.

People often eat outside when it is sunny. They may take picnics to the park or to the beach. A barbecue is an easy way to cook outside.

Water sports on vacation in the sunshine can be a lot of fun.

The Sun can be very hot, and it can be hard to tell how strong the sunlight is, especially on a windy day. It is very important for people to protect themselves so they do not get sunburn.

How can people protect themselves from sunburn?

People should stay in the shade between 11 a.m. and 3 p.m., when the Sun is at its strongest. When outside, it is important to keep putting on sunscreen to protect the body from burning. Wearing a T-shirt, hat, and sunglasses also helps.

People should always use sunscreen to prevent sunburn.

11

Too little sunshine

In some countries, there is not much sunshine during part of the year—especially in the winter. Without sunshine, places feel much colder because there is less heat from the Sun to warm them up. Cold weather can cause problems. For example, it can be difficult to start a car on a very cold morning, so people in cold places often put their cars away in garages at night.

In northern places, such as Scandinavia, there is very little sunshine during the winter, with only a few hours of sunlight each day.

In cold countries, people find ways to stay warm. They build houses that are well **insulated** and have **central heating**. They wear lots of layers of warm clothes. They might not spend as much time outside. In Chicago, Illinois, people have built lots of sidewalks underground, so they can walk around the city without going out into the cold.

Tents made using reindeer skins keep the Nenet people in Siberia in Russia, warm, despite the freezing temperatures.

Unbelievable!

At the **North Pole**, the Sun does not rise above the **horizon** for six months of the year! It stays dark for most of this time. For the other six months, the Sun does not sink below the horizon, so it stays light most of the time.

13

Is sunshine useful?

People make use of sunshine in different ways. Farmers need the Sun's light and heat so that grass will grow for their animals to eat. Crops also grow and ripen in the sunshine during the summer months. Farmers then harvest them at the start of the fall, when the weather begins to cool.

Farmers need sunshine to grow crops, such as wheat.

People use the sunshine to dry fruit and fish, to make these foods last longer. For example, raisins are made in California, by drying grapes in the sunshine.

People's bodies need a little bit of sunshine to make Vitamin D. Vitamin D helps people to have healthy bones, and it protects them from some illnesses, too.

Can the Sun tell the time?

A sundial can show the time using the Sun. A sundial has marks, like a clock, that show the hours of the day. It has a pointer called a gnomon. The gnomon blocks the direct light from the Sun to create a shadow. People can tell the time depending on where the shadow falls on the sundial.

Spending some time in the sunshine can help people to keep fit and healthy.

Sun energy

Electricity is a form of **energy**. People all around the world use electricity every day. Without it, lights, televisions, computers, and many other items would not work.

The heat and light from the Sun have a lot of energy. People can use this energy to make electricity. They use **solar panels** to change sunlight into electricity.

Food is cooked on solar stoves in many hot countries. The stoves are powered by the Sun.

Some people have small solar panels on the roofs of their houses, to make electricity for their homes. In some places, there are huge solar **power plants**, which make electricity for use in towns and cities. Many solar power plants are found in hot places, such as deserts, where there is plenty of sunshine.

Sunshine will always be important for life on Earth. In the future, we may be able to use sunshine even more. Some scientists think that, one day, we will be able to get most of our electricity from the Sun.

Unbelievable!

If people could capture all the sunlight that reaches the Earth in just 40 minutes, it could provide enough energy for the whole world for one year.

A large solar power plant can provide electricity to thousands of homes.

Too much sunshine

Some places can have too much sunshine. A heat wave is period of hot, sunny weather that lasts for longer than usual. Heat waves can happen almost anywhere, but they happen regularly in Africa, North and South America, Asia, and Australia.

In a heat wave, the Sun's heat dries out the ground. Plants may die, because they do not have enough water. Sometimes, trees and plants become so dry that they easily catch fire. Animals and people can die in forest fires, so the fire department tries to put out the fires very quickly.

A forest fire can quickly become out of control.

In a heat wave, people can get too hot. They may get heatstroke. This is when someone feels dizzy and sick because of the heat. People may sometimes need to go to the hospital with heatstroke. In extreme cases, people can die during a heat wave if they get too hot.

Unbelievable!

The longest heat wave in the world was at Marble Bar, Australia, in 1923–24. The temperature there was almost 100 degrees Fahrenheit (38 degrees Celsius) for more than 160 days!

Drinking lots of water can help to prevent heatstroke.

What is a drought?

A drought is a long period of time with very little rain. Often, droughts last for several months, but they can last for years. Droughts can happen all over the world.

The Atacama Desert, Chile, gets only 0.6 inches (1.5 centimeters) of rain a year.

 **Are there places that often have droughts?**

Some places have a lot of droughts. Since the 1970s, Ethiopia, Africa, has had a drought every few years. The worst one was in 1984–85, when about 800,000 people died.

Droughts usually happen because of changes in the weather. Some droughts happen because there is not as much rain as usual. Sometimes, this happens because the wind, which would normally bring rain, changes direction.

Droughts can also be caused by humans. People use water for drinking and bathing. Sometimes, people use so much water that it starts to run out, especially when there is less rain.

Droughts affect plants, animals, and people. All need water to survive. When there is less water during a drought, they may die.

If a drought takes place, this river could dry up, leaving no water to drink or to wash clothes or cook with.

Living with drought

Droughts affect people in different ways.
In some countries, such as the United States,
a drought may mean that people have to try to
save water. They may not be allowed to water
their yards. They may have to cut down
on activities such as water sports, because
lakes and rivers no longer hold enough water.

This crop of corn has been damaged by a drought.

Droughts have a damaging effect on farmers. With too little rain, their crops may die. Their animals may die, too, because there is not enough water for them to drink or food for them to eat.

During long droughts, there can be **famines**. This is when a large number of people do not have enough to eat. They become very thin and sick, or even die, because there is not enough to eat or there is no clean drinking water.

In hot places, such as Africa, thousands of people may starve during a famine caused by drought.

Unbelievable!

The longest-ever drought, in the Atacama Desert, Chile, lasted for 400 years, from 1571 to 1971.

Dealing with drought

In a poor country, the **government** does not have enough money to help all the people who have been affected by a drought. There might be millions of people who are hungry or sick. Farmers may need help to plant new crops or to buy food for their animals.

Often, richer countries provide help. Governments and **aid agencies** give whatever is needed, such as money and food. In 2003, aid agencies helped over 13 million Ethiopians affected by drought.

Aid agencies set up temporary camps in which they provide people with food during droughts.

Some countries, such as the United States, U.K., and Australia, help to improve people's access to water in poor places. This can protect people from the worst effects of drought. In parts of Africa, millions of dollars have been spent on **wells** and **reservoirs**.

Unbelievable!

In China, scientists can make rain! They use a process called "cloud seeding." Chemicals are fired into the sky in rockets, or are dropped from a plane. These chemicals change in the clouds to make rain for areas affected by drought.

Water stored in a well can give people a reliable source of water to survive a drought.

Planning ahead

The best way for people to prepare for a drought is to make the water they have last longer. Water can be easily saved at home by taking a shower instead of a bath, or by turning the faucet off when brushing teeth or washing dishes.

Rainwater is collected whenever it falls in many hot countries, to prepare for times when rain is scarce.

If farmers expect a dry year, they can plant crops that need less water to grow. They can also save some of last year's crop, so they have **seeds** to plant or eat if a drought does come.

In very hot countries, **indigenous** people often know the places they can find water underground or from plants. Scientists have found ways to change saltwater into water that is safe to drink.

Saving seeds at harvest time can help farmers to prepare for a drought.

 ? How much water do people use?

People use water at home, for farming, and for **industry**. People in rich countries use much more water than people in poor countries. In parts of the U.S.A., one person uses 264 gallons (1,000 liters) of water every day. In parts of Africa, one person only uses 26 gallons (10 liters) of water daily.

Measuring temperature

Use a thermometer to measure the temperature in different parts of a building. You can then record your results on a chart and compare them.

1. Draw a plan of your house. Mark the bathroom, kitchen, and yard with an X. You will measure temperature in these areas.

2. Copy the chart below onto a piece of paper. You will record your findings on this chart.

Area	Bathroom	Yard	Kitchen
Temperature 1			
Temperature 2			
Difference in temperature			
Reason for difference			

3. Place the thermometer in the bathroom. **before** you have a shower. Record the temperature. Take a shower and record the temperature again.

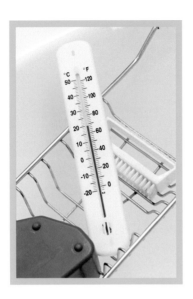

4. Place the thermometer in the yard. After a few minutes, record the temperature. After three hours, record the temperature again.

5. Place the thermometer in the kitchen, **before** a meal is cooked. Record the temperature. Once the meal is cooked, record the temperature again.

6. Now compare the difference between the two temperatures for each area. Was there a change between your first and second reading? Why do you think this was? Record your reasons.

Understanding your findings

1. Hot water from your shower warmed the bathroom air. This made the temperature rise.

2. If you took your second reading in the yard after noon, warmth from the Sun may have made the temperature rise.

If you took the second reading toward late afternoon or evening, the Sun's rays would have been weaker and the temperature may have fallen.

3. Heat from the oven or stove warmed the kitchen. This made the temperature rise.

Glossary

aid agencies organizations that provide help, such as money or food, to people who need it

air conditioning system to keep the air in a building cool

central heating way of heating a building, for example, with radiators

electricity form of energy that powers machines

energy power, such as electricity, which is used to work machines

famines when there is very little or no food to eat

government group of people who run a country

horizon line in distance where the sky seems to touch land or sea

indigenous naturally existing in a place, rather than coming from somewhere else

industry activities that produce items for sale

insulated covered or surrounded with special materials to stop heat from escaping

North Pole area on the Earth that is farthest north

power plants factories that create energy

reservoirs places where rainwater is stored

seasons parts of the year. Spring, summer, fall, and winter are all seasons

seeds small parts of a plant. New plants grow from planted seeds

solar panels objects that change the Sun's energy into electricity

wells deep holes in the ground from which water can be taken

Further Information and Web Sites

Books

Earth's Weather and Climate
by Jim Pipe (Gareth Stevens Publishing, 2008)

Energy Sources: Solar Power
by Neil Morris (Smart Apple Media, 2006)

Harnessing Power From The Sun
by Niki Walker (Crabtree Publishing, 2007)

Web Sites

Due to the changing nature of Internet links, PowerKids Press has developed an online list of Web sites related to the subject of this book. This site is updated regularly. Please use this link to access this list:
http://www.powerkidslinks.com/wwise/sun/

Index